Selection of

Poems

and

Short Stories

MAREE ALAINA GRAHAM

Paperback: 978-1-959224-36-5
eBook: 978-1-959224-37-2
Library of Congress Control Number: 2022923793

Ordering Information:

Prime Seven Media
518 Landmann St.
Tomah City, WI 54660

Printed in the United States of America

Table of Contents

About the Author

I was born in Sydney Australia. I am a Mother and a Nana. Twice divorced. I am with a wonderful man David, he is number three we have been together for twenty eight years. We appreciate each other and accept each other totally.

Throughout my life I have been; at different times on emotional roller coasters. Trying to balance home life and work. Without much support.

Of course I was not the only one in this predicament, many women were in the same boat. My family was not pleased with me when I divorced my first husband, it was not the one thing in those days. One was to supposed to stay married not matter what! The second divorce shocked everyone." He seemed so nice or he was such a hard worker"! The old saying of "street angel home devil" was spot on with this man. A man he was not. These failed relationships sent me on a mission to discover me. I learned that all the things that happen in life good or not can either make us stronger or we can fall into a heap and stay there.

I began to write how I felt and was surprised at how angry I was, I had lost faith in myself completely. Two failed marriages my daughter hated me, my family disappointed in me. Why in the hell was I even alive!

I read all the books on self-esteem and letting go and being responsible for one own life.

The bottom line for me was forgiving myself for the rotten decisions I made I learned never to make a decision when in an emotional state. Then I wrote down on a piece of paper the kind of man (if there was one) I'd like in my life. Then put it away and forgot about it.

I stopped making excuses for my life being such a failure and began making changes.

As well as working in Nursing Homes as an Assistant Nurse I also went to evening college to become a Qualified Massage and Reflexology Therapist, then studied counseling and became qualified in that area too.

I was able to assist other people who had similar life problems as I had.

Then I met the David, he taught me how to laugh again and he was all that I said I wanted.

My poems and my stories are about life, not just mine, they are from those whom I have observed. They are from the many wonderful people I have met, their hopes and dreams. Sometimes my poems are about how we wished our lives could have been.

The most important thing I learned is without these experiences I would never have become who I am today.

It is my wish that those who read this book to find something of value in it that may indeed bring about change.

Acknowledgements

The Images are from Microsoft Home Publishing 2000.

To Tiffany Cooper a busy mum with four children a husband and a business to organize and still found the time to draw pictures for the Willy Stories.

To David my partner for all the cups of tea, the dinners and the encouragement to continue.

To Joan who has always delighted to read what I had written.

A big thank you to you all.

Poems

Dedication.

This is dedicated to the Grandparents whose time is limited.
This poem is about my granddaughters.
The distance between us being too far, my work load too long,
The visits too few.
I would think of them before going to sleep, and the stories I
Would tell them when I could visit.
Although they had many books,
They always wanted the ones in my head

Ame and Elise.

I have two little granddaughters, Ame and Elise.
I visit them every night, while they are sound asleep.
Tiptoeing very quietly so no one knows I am there,
I whisper very softly how much their Nana cares.

Sometimes I tell them stories of fairies having fun,
Or tell them of the Daffodils that jump out of the garden and run.
They like the one of the boy in the moon, he makes the
      Stars come out.
If they listen very carefully, they will hear him sing and
      shout, "Come on stars shine real bright" and then he
      zooms away.

As a smile appears on their faces, I watch in sheer delight.
      Oh, what a glorious sight!
As morning fast approaches, their Nana cannot stay,
and whispers very softly, "Have a wonderful day"

Fiercely Independent.

I am fiercely, I can do many things
like chopping wood or cutting grass.
I don't sit around and let things pass.

I can even get the barbie going,
A true Aussie woman I am.
Washing, cooking, cleaning the house,
Taking good care of my spouse.

I am fiercely independent.

I taught myself how to use a computer,
That was quite a task,
For there was absolutely no one I could ask.
It took some time but I figured it out,
I thought I was pretty smart.
I am fiercely independent.

Then I bought a mobile phone.
With my spouse working away,
It would come in mighty handy
We could talk every day.

Visiting my daughter she greeted me and said,

"Mum you've got to learn how to text"
"It would be really good if you could show me
just how it is done,".
"I don't have time mum, I'm sure you'll figure it out."
Then she walked away.
I was getting a little perplexed with trying to "figure" it out.

I threw the thing on the floor, then went outside for a while.
Oh yes I am fiercely independent,
I thought I was pretty smart......until.

Then my four year old granddaughter said,
"Nana don't be sad, I can show you the easy way,
Daddy taught me how.

Her little fingers went so fast, my eyes could not keep up.
My daughter laughing hysterically at the stunned look on my face.

Eventually I did get it, thought it took a bit of time.
I surely made many mistakes giving up was not on my mind,
Oh, I would much rather have a chat or even write a letter!
I am fiercely independent, I will practice until I get better.

This is dedicated to my Nana, she made the best apple pies.
I have never tasted any apple pie anywhere as good.
Many years have passed since my Nana passed away,
I can still remember how good her apple pies tasted.

Happy Apple Pie.

Homegrown apples fresh as can be,
Children picking them playfully.
Hurry, hurry, lots to do.
Get them back to Nana to stew.

Off to church, say our prayers,
rush back home and up the stairs.
Change our clothes rush back down,
Whip the cream, our little heart pound!

Then waiting for the dinner call, we wash our hands,
Manners galore.
Meat and veggies come out first,
Children smiling ready to burst!

"Careful now it's very hot"
Lashings of cream and custard too,
Happy Apple pie we are ready for you.

This poem is about the many wonderful moments with my mother.

Nothing ever phased her.

Five children a husband, cats, dogs and birds,

Nothing was too much trouble.

She was an amazing woman.

I never became a doctor. I did however become a qualified Assistant Nurse and other health therapies followed.

A Moment.

Wipe the tears from your eye's little girl,
    a broken doll can be mended.
A doll so loved from Santa Clause,
    shared with a puppy.

Arms and legs all torn off, the insides were all out.
The doll was such a mess, the little girl cries and shouts.

Some cotton, a needle a thimble too carried in on a tray.
The operation of "fix her please, can you do it today"?

The little girl watches her mother use tender loving care.
    The rag doll put back together.
    A precious moment shared.

The little girl grew up and became a doctor. Putting people
    back together.
And remembers a time with her mother that stayed with her
    forever.

December 2016

Little Black Bear

I watched a Television program about bears from around the world

Their treatment was appalling. I turned the television off. I went to bed feeling very sad, and I dreamed about a little black bear.

I jumped out of bed at 2am and wrote this poem down.

The Little Black Bear

He sat in a cage tube hanging out,

Men in white coats and polished shoes all about.

No one noticed the tear run down the snout

Of a frightened little black bear.

If he could speak he would say" this is no way

For man to behave, I cannot make you better"

This little black bear has not long to live.

As the juices of his life are taken from him.

As man pats himself on the back,

Potions made to sell and make money.

No one seems to care as a little black bear closes his eyes, all of nature begin to cry

Something beautiful has just died.

Dedication for When Love Dies.

This poem is dedicated to my daughter Georgina,
Who left home to find herself and succeeded.

To all the daughters that leave home and to the
mothers who let them.

To the celebration of the heart when love returns.

When Love Dies.

On the day my daughter was born, I was overjoyed.
　　To her father I made two mistakes.
　　　I did not have a boy.
　　Why did I have her the day before his birthday!
　　　Surely I could have waited!

It was beyond my control I said.
　　He did not believe me.
As he held her in his arms he said he was only joking.
　　Next time you will get it right
There is no doubt about it.

What an emotional train I was on,
　　I knew it could not last.
My daughter and I were both wounded
　　as this marriage slipped into the past.

I married again, this second one was worse that the first,
　　Though in the beginning it was fine.
It took a long time to get over it,
　　More scars for this daughter of mine.

I slipped into depression….I couldn't cope with such pain!
　　Deceived, destroyed, my emotions shot to pieces,
　　　I will never marry again!

My daughter and I began to grow apart,
  We could not please each other,
    I was always wrong,
    She was never right.
I was fearful when she did not come home at night.

  Her music gave me a headache,
    My music made her sick.
We did not like each other not even a little bit.

  Marrying young, she moved away.
  We barely contacted each other,
  When we did our words were harsh,
  It was clear we were still hurting.

I thought this is how it was meant to be,
there was no love between my daughter and me.
Somehow in our sorrow it seemed love just died.
Many nights I could not sleep…many nights I cried.

Then some years down the track she had a daughter of her own,
A broken marriage, counselling too,
Just like her mother had to do, letting go of the past.

Learning about emotions, moving away from the dark,
    Wounds healed, lessons learned.
    Finding self-worth again.
    We both got off an emotional train,
    A whole lot wiser; so much gained.
Accepting each other and not playing the blame game.

Come hold my hand.

Come hold my hand my old friend, walk with me a while.
Let us go down to the Lake, have a nice cup of tea and a piece of
      cake.
We can take our time, no need to rush. We have all the time in
      the world.
Talking about how times have changed and indeed people too.

Laughing at the silly things we used to do.
Collecting tadpoles, climbing trees, they were but a few.
Remember the subjects we had to learn in school.
How to cook and the importance of reading books.

Respecting our parents was high on the list,
I remember the day I told my mother to hush
When I got up from the floor my father told me
If I ever spoke to her like that again I would be out the door!

How life has changed my old friend, there is not so much
      thinking today,
It's oh so easy put the computer on most answers are already there.
I wonder what happens to the brain that doesn't think,
Does it stop functioning or does it just sit.
To figure things out all by oneself has a certain sense of pride
      and self-esteem.

*We must do this again my friend, we have so much to talk
about and the day is at an end.
Next time we will go to the beach and sit on the warm sand,
We'll talk about dancing all night, missing the last train and
the long walk home.*

Come hold my hand.

I stepped outside, I could smell the rain coming.
Clouds were beginning to gather;
I noticed a little dark cloud all by itself.
Bigger clouds began to move closer to the little cloud.
Thunder began it's rolling sound across the sky.
Then I saw lightning go right through the little dark cloud.

I wondered what it thought.

My First Memory

It was black all around me as far as could be seen. 1 was safe in knowing no harm could come to me.

Then it happened without warning. A bolt of light went through me,

The noise deafening!

I was so frightened I began to cry uncontrollably,

I heard sounds unfamiliar to me, trying to remember what it was, searched my memory

Then a voice familiar spoke to me and told me these sounds were laughter. I was distraught, laughter, who would be laughing at my tears!

People, you have made people happy" was the reply

I did not understand.

The voice laughed again and replied, "You are a storm cloud, your tears have broken a long drought. Now crops will grow and gardens flourish and flowers will bloom"

Your tears are called Rain and I am Lightening, it is my job to make you cry, together you and I bring life to this planet."

Now I was satisfied knowing my first memory was tears.

This is a humorous look of searching our past to confirm we
all have ancestors,
The shock we may feel when we find out where we came from
and who we are related to.
I remember reading a book some time ago of the ancestral line
of an "Upper Class Lady" and the last line of the last page the
young Lady says
"I am so glad I am not related to such heathens"!
          Our beginnings were not so good.
We can only do better for our future. Leave the past where it is.

My Family Tree.

From Eric the Red to a King of Scotland.
A Lord and Lady in London.
Barbarians, Royalty and god knows what.
I cringe at the thought of such a horrible lot!

My ancestors were violent or so I am told,
Strong and aggressive and very bold.
Some lost their heads, some died in their beds,
No convicts as such, not that it matters much.

How can this be, that someone as nice as me.
Can have such a family history!
Now all that belongs in the past, it just could not last.
I really don't care, I wasn't there.
I am sure someone must have been better.

What part would I be on the family tree?
Just a bit of rotten old wood!
I will chop it down and start again,
So future generations can see the beginning started with me
And think their ancestors were lovely.

Dedicated to All the Happy Children

This poem came into my mind as I was walking through a park.
Children were playing as their parents were talking.
I thought wouldn't it be nice if their parents joined in too.

Children

Children's laughter and their games,
can teach adults to love the rain.
Take time out to join in too,
show your children fun things to do.

Like secrets hidden in the garden,
Flowers blooming and bees are buzzing.
Turn the soil watch the worms.
Funny faces bodies squirm.

Listen to their bedtime prayers,
Settle them down with a teddy bear.
Take an interest in all they do,
Get excited with them at the Zoo.

Give them all the love you can,
in the years that they are very young.
Nurturing, guidance, some discipline too,
Teach your children what they CAN do.

The answer to questions they want to know
Just how does a garden grow?
Is it the worms, the rain and the sun?
Perhaps, it's the sound of children having fun.

Jacaranda Tree Dedication

I just love the way they display themselves,
they are poems waiting to happen.

The Jacaranda Tree.

Lilac flowers greet the day,
Jacarandas on display.
Branches stretching far and wide,
Bringing life, standing with pride.

Covering footpaths with their little bells;
Who would complain, who would tell.
The Jacaranda only knows
How to bloom and how to grow.

The Lemon Tree

My partner and I rented a house in the suburb of Northmead.

On a good day it was a twenty minute drive to Sydney.

The house was an old fibro, very hot in Summer and freezing in Winter.

Living next door was an elderly Lady, Joan and her son Mark.

We became good friends, Joan had lost her daughter to cancer, I guess I filled in.

In her backyard was a sorrowful looking lemon tree. It had lots of lemons but only one or two were any good. So many on the ground.

Joan told me when her husband was alive he would look after it, Her son was not interested in any kind of gardening. So the poor tree only got watered when it rained.

That's sad Joan, lemons are so expensive to buy these days.

Well that night and the following four or five nights I would dream about this Lemon tree. It was usually a vibrant colour loaded with juicy lemons. It was really weird, there was a face in the tree and it would say "help me" it reminded me of the old movie "The Fly"

Finally I asked Joan if she minded if I looked after her tree, Her reply was that would be wonderful, I'd do it myself but it's too big.

At the weekend I set about pruning the tree, my partner dug up around the base of the tree and cleared all the grass and weeds

It was a few weeks before it started producing good juicy lemons.

That night I dreamed of the lemon tree again and the face in it was happy and said Thank you.

It's funny how some plants communicate with us humans.

My partner and I moved to a Rural area it was sad for Joan and me too.

Joan loved listening to me read my poems, she cried when I read "The little Black Bear" and she cried when I read "The Bracelet"

Sadly in 2016 Joan passed away. In 2020 her house was knocked down for development and the lemon tree was dug up and thrown away.

I never dreamed of the Lemon Tree again.

The Nature of Poems Dedication

This poem is about how we often think we "can't"
Then surprise ourselves when we can.

The Nature of Poems

Poems are like songs without music they come right from the heart. Putting together the magic of words is one of the finer arts.

To tell of the future or the past, then write it down in verse. Creating an abundance of beauty for all who enjoy the written word.

To pick up a pen, to put it on paper with not a thought in your head. As strange as that seems, it's like that for me... and then it just happens.

Words, words, beautiful words arrange themselves just right. Funny sad good or bad,

The poems tell a tale of life.

Trains & Boats & Planes Dedication

Waiting all year for a holiday.
On the day we are ready to leave down came the rain.
That was here and we were going elsewhere.
Nothing was going to stop our holiday!

Note:
Circular Quay in Sydney, Australia, is pronounced "Key"

Trains & Boats & Planes.

We ran for the train in the pouring rain,
  a holiday we had planned.
We arrived at Circular Quay where our boat
  would be to take us to Tahiti.
While there we planned to see the sights.
We slept during the day and partied all night.

The weather was great, we made new friends,
  we were having so much fun,
We did not want this holiday to end.

We joined a group to travel far,
  boarding a plane that had a bar!
Exotic drinks and singing too.
The pilot got a headache and so did the crew.
We did not care we had even forgotten we were in the air.

When the plane landed, we were all tipsy.
We had our fortune told by a Gypsy.
She said she could "see" wonderful things for my friends and me.
Assuring us this was no game.
I "see" around you travel on trains and boats and planes.

This Planet Earth Dedication

I am passionate about this planet, it is so beautiful

Mother nature knows exactly how it all works.

What madness makes "man" want to destroy it!

This earth belongs to all of us,

Everything we need is here.

Why is it not enough!

This Planet Earth.

Who really cares who or what created this earth world.
          I only know I am a part of it.
At night I get excited looking at the stars,
          with no thought of any life beings on Mars.
The Moon tonight is full and glowing with pride,
          taking the night in its stride.
No concerns as to where it will shine,
I have none either for tonight this Moon is mine.

The Moon watches as its power changes the weather,
          especially the tides from calm to wild.
All of nature responds and understands,
          except of course MAN!
He is too busy looking into space,
spending billions of dollars hoping to find
a new planet where he can control the people
          destroy and dominate!
The billion of dollars wasted probing space
          is a disgrace, when it could
be spent to educate, to teach the people how to survive.
To become custodians of this earth.
This....planet....earth....is....all......there....is!

Life won't be found "there" until life is respected here!

Until Governments learn to speak the truth,

and people learn to care about each other.

If there is another Race of people in space, I am sure we have
had a visit.

They probably whizzed around when no one was around,
taking a film of the damage already done, and how no
wars are ever won.

Like all intelligent beings who travel through space....
they left!

She and the Sea is dedicated to the many women and young girls who have had emotional trauma at some point in their lives. Left alone or abandoned, unable to find a way out.

This is a poem of love and hope.

She and the Sea.

She stood facing the sea feeling alone as could be.

Where did she go so long ago, could she find herself here?

The struggle to live to receive to give, sorrow was now overflowing.

In her tormented mind was a child whose laughter was once a joy.

This child who was forever finding all sorts of little treasures.

The hopes and dreams for this child to have a future filled with pleasures.

Love was given then taken away, too many times her heart was broken.

She had decided to end it all.

Into the sea she walked with no thoughts of returning.

Her spirit and soul had both been destroyed,

What did she have to live for.

She had no tears, she did not blame, she was not after pity nor seeking fame.

No one knew of the battles she had won; there was no record of her achievements.

She walked into the sea knowing there would be no one to grieve,

A tidal wave began to form, her emotions created a storm!

Then a wave scooped her up gently and firmly extending with precision and might.

Safely returning her to the beach close to midnight.

Somewhere deep within she knew life was not finished with her yet.

She had nothing to give, no reason to live.

A voice she heard outside her ear, spoke to her with much

Love.

This voice knew her name, it moved her so, dried up tears

began to flow.

Never had she felt like this, she did not understand.

"It's not your time, you cannot die," this voice was like no other.

"A child is waiting to be born, and has chosen you for its

mother."

Dedicated to those who have suffered with depression

Everyone has a different opinion on just what depression is. There are many medications, groups, and therapists too. All of them have value

For me however I thought it all was a cover up, I didn't want to cover it up I wanted it gone!

I am not qualified in Mental Health. This is from my experience only, I believe it starts with the emotions and turns into **Emotional Depression.**

Think about that for a moment and see how you feel. On the brink of ending my life, I found that it is the simplest things that work best.

So I spoke to my brain and also my mind, I told them to quit lazing around and show me something **I could do.**

That night I had a dream that I was playing golf (I hate golf) and written on the balls were negative words, heavy words, Fear, Failure Grief, Sadness, Hopelessness and many others.

There were hundreds of balls. I was hitting them in all directions, mostly missing them and they stayed at my feet. Boy was I getting angry.

When I woke up I thought about the dream, and decided to do it again this time I saw myself on a tennis court whacking those balls out of sight!

I turned on the radio and they were playing......" They're Coming to take Me Away Ha Ha" I laughed so much I cried.

To all who suffer with depression and think there is no way out.......there is.

It is my wish you too will discover that there are many miracles in life, and the best one is you, so be kind to yourself and you too will find your way out.

Leave Me Alone.

Leave me alone, I'm so depressed,
I don't have the strength to get out of bed.
Nor do I want to get dressed,
Night and day have become the same, I sleep!

This heaviness is too much to bare, I cannot seem to escape it.
No one really knows how I feel, many give me advice with their
        kind words,
" Get over it!"
I am slipping down, I've lost control.

Every night I asked for a solution, no answer do I get.
Crying at the drop of a hat, this is so damn boring.

Days, weeks and months go by. This life of mine is a failure.
I start to plan how I will end it and be done with the pain I am in.

Oh no, just a minute something I forgot,
Who will take care of my flowers, I'll have to sort that out.

I make it out to my garden, I hadn't seen it for months, standing
        there in disbelief, tears flowing down my cheeks.
My beautiful flowers were hidden under so much grass and
        weeds, my garden was so neglected.
This garden was a reflection of me.

Gloves on my hands hat on my head, I knelt down in front of my garden bed.

Working all day until it was done, oh my goodness they are all there.

I watered them down and was pleased with myself, then I whispered "I'm so sorry. I will never let this happen again."

Walking away it started to rain. A bonus for my flowers.

Coming towards me was a old man, with a big smile on his face.

"They would not have lived much longer Miss I'm glad to see you out and about, you have given these flowers a second chance."

Then he said something I will never forget.

"I've come to give you a message, when you die make sure you are happy, then the destination will be more than you hoped for"

Then he vanished right before my eyes.

A feeling of love flowed through me and I suddenly felt quite light,

The flowers in my garden were looking oh so bright.

This poem is dedicated to all volunteers,
Who work tirelessly giving their time unconditionally.
Showing the gift of human kindness, they are indeed very
Special people.

Many organizations could not survive without them.

Human Kindness.

Human kindness overflows in many wonderful ways.
We only see it when disasters strike.
Yet it works during the day and all night.

Volunteers' workers help those in need, not caring about colour
or creed.

Their payment is in how good it makes them feel, knowing the
difference they have made to the life of another human being.

So when you fall down and think you can't go on,
Take a look around and you will surely see,
The hands of human kindness are reaching out to thee.

Life continually changes just like the seasons.
Teenagers living the wild life, burning the candle at both ends.
Parents trying to stop them from getting hurt.

Some things do not change, all that parents can hope for,
Is that their children will survive the teenage years.
Just as they did.

Changes.

History repeats itself over and over again.
Wars, killings, hatreds and crimes.
Abusing children, beating wives.

This is nothing new!

Teenagers get drunk, take drugs break the law,
drive fast cars, some teenagers, not all.
The young think this is fun,
believing they are bullet proof!
Ain't that the truth.

This is nothing new!

Each generation will be the same.
Thinking it's something new.
How quickly adults forget that
THEY WERE TEENAGERS TOO!

This is a tongue in cheek look at the behavior of
        Politicians.
It is my opinion, that politicians need to behave
        a bit better.
It would be so nice if they could stop digging up the dirt
on each other, trying to make the other side look bad,
        so they can look good.
Perhaps if they could leave their egos at home along with
their childish behavior and get on with each other,
then perhaps the country would be in a better state.
They might even find they enjoy it.
        I know the people certainly would.

The Politicians School.

If you want to be a politician, you'll need to go to a special school.
Learning to be a part of a government, or perhaps a leader would suit'
In this school you will learn how to look a person in the eyes, keep a straight face while telling them lies.

 Truth is never an option here.
 You must never admit to fault.
Treat all people equally, except if they are poor.

You'll learn to bandy with words like Racism and see what that conjures up.
Then bring in political correctness, and other useless stuff.
Comedians find this quite a pain!
As do the rest of us.

People have always made fun at each other, and made fun at themselves.
This is not confined to one country, this is all around the world!
Comedians make a living by getting people to laugh at the way countries are being run.
How politicians stuff it up, cover it up then flee.

Well now, I don't mind if you make fun of me, it's perfectly alright.
At least it has got you laughing, now doesn't that feel good.
Politicians lighten up, relax a little bit.

You are making life too serious, you're making people sick!
Staying awake trying to think of ways to take away freedom.
You believe no one else knows how to think!

Seeing right through the veils of deceit, people are not blinded by the lies.
We know it's about building up the coffers, by taxing us to death.
Paying for parking on the streets that we have already paid for.
Paying for roads, then paying to use them, then paying to park at the beach.!

What a cheek!
The only time you are halfway nice is at Election time.
With promises to right the wrongs the "other" side has made.
It takes courage, strength to be a good leader.
That is not taught in your school.
Nor is charity begins at home, taking care of your own,
Helping the people that live on the streets.
Showing some respect to all.

Each country must do the same, then you can help your neighbours,
That's the way it is meant to be,
Perhaps one day leaders from all over the world will learn to work together.
I am sure you will find, people will begin to be kind.
When Leaders find the courage they can change it for the better.

My Sister Fay Dedication

This poem is in itself a dedication to my big sister.
Supporting me in so many ways throughout my life.

My Sister Fay

I don't like the title sibling,
It's a word I find unappealing.
Fay is my sister, my friend and more.
Always there when needed.
She may appear frail its true,
There is not much Fay cannot do.

With her family her strength can be seen,
By her loving her caring and patience.
Whether its Reiki or Bowen, Fay gives one hundred
percent, treating people until they are well.
If Reiki or Bowen does not suit,
She will offer them some fresh fruit.
A cup of tea and conversation.

Fay does not gossip or criticize,
Or worry about futile things.
She is a beacon of light that shines bright,
My sister Fay is a unique human being.

Words can't express my gratitude
For all that Fay has done.
Her uncanny knowing when things were not right.
Even when we are miles apart,
My sister Fay is in my heart.

The Middle Sister.

The middle sister she has always been.
Lynette is her name.
A wild child she was, never one for games,
So very different from my older sister and me.
I used to torment her so.

I love her more than I did before,
I accept her just as she is.
That usually happens the older one gets,
Looking at life differently.

Lynette worked so hard throughout her life,
Looking after her family, paying for a house.
Today Lynette has retired from work,
No, she doesn't sit around.

Out and about playing sports and even in a choir,
Lynette is living her life to the fullest.
That's always been her desire.

The Bushman Dedication

This poem is dedicated to all the men and women,
Who have fought and died for freedom.
To those who are still fighting for freedom.
To the families who wait for their return.
The price of freedom is high.
Let us all respect it and give thanks.

The Bushman

Tom stoked the fire with a piece of wood,
his cooked rabbit looked mighty good.
With veggies and gravy, he enjoyed so.
He had learned to cook many years ago.
Tom sat by the fire and lit his pipe,
poured a cup of coffee as he did every night.

He heard a rustle in the bush and slowly turned around,
The bush at night was a different world, filled with many sounds.
Looking rather nervous was a young man and his wife.
Introducing themselves, they said they wanted to experience
bush life.

"Folks in town said maybe you'd enjoy some company, we
only have a week"
"I don't mind at all, said Tom, would you like coffee or tea?"
They asked him many questions, they were keen to know,
Why he chose to live in the bush. Why he loves it so.

"I fought in wars for freedom, said Tom, at least that's what I thought,
I watched my mates die; I saw things that made me cry.
Things that will not leave me."

Tom sighed, "There was one thing that kept me sane,
Through the misery and the pain, a poetry book my mother
        gave to me."
"Did you have a favourite one Tom?" the young man asked.
Without hesitation Tom replied.
"To a Skylark, by Percy Bysshe Shelly, born 1792 and died
in 1882.
His poems were quite long, but I loved every word."

"Then when the fighting was over and some of us came home.
I for one could not settle down, there was no trauma counselling
        then, not like there is today.
We were expected to behave like nothing had ever happened!
The city was too noisy, cars beeping their horns made me
Feel like I was back in the war.
So, I kissed my mother on her cheek and shook my fathers hand.
I said I gotta get out of here, I am going bush for a couple years.

I met up with my Mate Charlie, who was pretty much like me,
Together we started roaming this beautiful country."
The young man asked what the war was like, Tom was taken
        aback.
He did not like talking about it for it made him feel sad.
"There is only one thing you need to know, and for both sides
        it's the same.
Women lose their husbands, sons, their life.
War it a futile game."

"Where is Charlie now?" asked the young wife, changing the subject.

"Charlie stayed a couple of years; he missed the city life.

We lost contact with each other; I have not seen him for years '

The week went by too quickly, the young couple had to return
    to the city.

Tom quite liked their company and thought their leaving was a
    pity.

They promised they would return as soon as they could, there
    was still much more for them to learn.

True to their word the young couple returned after two months
    had passed.

They were keen to see Tom again.

Stopping in town and were sad to hear.

Old Tom was not around, he had died in Spring.

Under his favourite Blue Gum tree.

In his lap, they were told, was a book of poetry,

opened at the last verse of Shellys "To a Skylark"

This poem is dedicated to the many senior citizens in Nursing Homes.

All have a story to tell, mostly they keep it to themselves.

Sometimes when the moment is right, they share the stories.

I consider myself very fortunate indeed to have been there to listen to them.

Charlie bought tears to me eyes.

Charlie.

Charlie sat in his wheelchair,
in a Veterans Nursing Home.
He never had any visitors,
Charlie was all alone.

Although his body was broken
his mind was sharp as a tack.
He looked like he carried the woes
of the world on his back.

I wheeled him outside to be in the fresh air,
peeling for him his favourite fruit, a juicy brown pear.
I noticed as he ate it in his eyes were tears.
"Why are you so sad Charlie?" I asked.
"I've lived long enough nurse, I wish I was dead,
please take me back to bed."

Charlie started to talk to me about things he wished
he had not done.
Like the day he left his young wife,' cause he couldn't
handle life.
"Coming home from the war, I just could not be still,
my continual pacing made my wife ill."

"I went bush with my mate Tom"
Charlie paused to wipe his tears.

"I stayed with him for a couple of years.
Then I yearned to go back home.
And left Tom all alone."

"Old Tom he liked poetry, he had a little book."
Charlie, on his face came a strange look.
"I still remember his favourite poem,
It was Shellys "To a Skylark"
We all knew it off by heart."

Charlie got his wish, on the first day of Spring,
Passing away in his sleep.
I will always remember a man named Charlie.

My Friend.

I leaned next to a tree of majestic size,
I'd heard it had stood here for 3 hundred years.
This tree was surely a prize.

I told this tree how beautiful it is
"You have the persona of woman a true goddess in every way.
Confident in what you are, & never do you question.
Your knowledge is your strength your truth.
No one would ever oppose you."

I felt its energy against my back,
So relaxed I fell asleep.
My dreams were peaceful
I felt safe.

In the blink of an eye I awoke with a start
To the sound of thunder and lightning
The rain bucketed down all around
There was nowhere for me to go.

Home was too far.....My mother had told me ....."
The weather out here is different my dear.....
It can change without warning....
So stay close to home.... I said yes!

Not a cloud in the sky, the sun was out there was plenty of time
to wander about!

I looked up into the tree the branches too high for me,

Thinking what was I going to do.....
A branch dropped down and I held on
tight as it picked me up and took me high.

Water rising and moving fast covering the dry land.
Not a drop touched me,
I was safe in this tree.

I could hear a helicopter flying overhead,
They could not see me
All they could see was this magnificent tree.

As the night slipped away, the storm did too
By morning the skies returned to a clear blue.

My father had come in his boat looking everywhere for me
He could not believe his eyes, when he found me
There I was sound asleep on the bough of this mighty tree with
its branches wrapped around me.

My father yelled to my brother Joe "Pass me the saw, this tree
wont let her go!"

I opened my eyes no worse for ware
Called to my father who was in despair
"No need for a saw, I am alright, this tree kept me safe all through
the night!"
The branch lowered me right into the boat,
My father wrapping me in his woolen coat.

To this day this tree still stands
Her mighty roots holding onto this land.

The secret of the Tree.

The tree stood proud and strong
It was at least ten men wide.
Branches long leaves golden green.
I was in awe of this beautiful tree.

As I moved closer I felt my energy soar,
From my toes to my head, is this real?
I felt truly alive and completely healed.

No aches or pain in this body of mine,
I had not felt this good for a very long time.

Moving into the tree.... YES right inside
In a wonderland.... Down the roots I did slide.
This way and that, round and round
Like the big dipper at Luna Park!
No fear of being alone in the dark
I was a happy as a lark!

How lucky am I to experience this
It can only be described as perfect bliss.
I felt the pulsating of the earth
Like it was getting ready to give birth.

There is so much more to a tree

More than the eyes can see.
For me through this journey into the tree
I now know there is much more.... to being me!
Much more than you will see!

Lasting Friendship.(c)

A friend knows not of distance or time,
Nor talking or meeting somewhere.
A friend that is true, has a place just for you,
Tucked away in the heart and the mind.

The years pass away, the body may change…
For some it's the body, for others the brain.
True friends remember each other's name.

As we mature, like a wonderful wine,
We make little notes to remind us.
True friends stand the test of time.

This Poem is dedicated to my friend Barbara.
Leaving Scotland with her two daughters to
settle in Australia and start a new life.
Barbara made her home in Penrith, where she taught Relaxacise,
A mixture of Yoga exercise and relaxation.
Barbara helped to change so many lives including mine.

We became instant friends. I learned so much from Barbara.
No matter how she felt, she would always greet me with a smile.
Barbara passed away before I could give her this Poem or to say
"Goodbye my friend and thank you."

Knowing Barbara was an honor and a privilege.

Short Stories

Willy The Worm

Willy The Worm

Part One

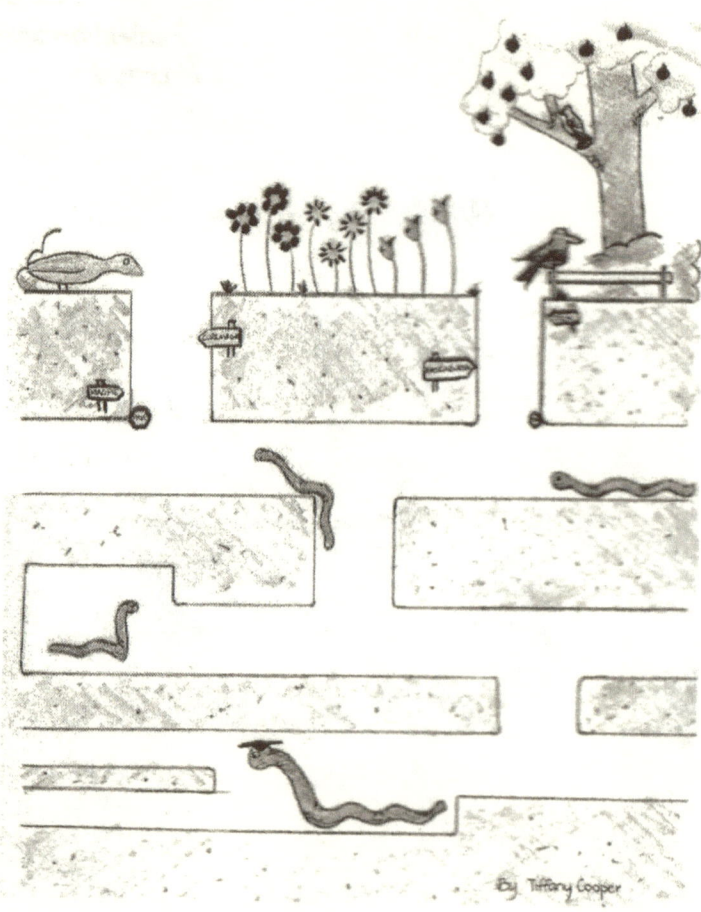

By Tiffany Cooper

Mrs MacGreggor had the finest flower and vegetable garden in the whole town. People came from everywhere to admire it Mrs Mac as she was affectionately called, spent most of her day pottering around her garden telling her flowers how beautiful they were, and her vegetables how good they looked.

The flowers responded displaying the most unusual colours with aroma that filled the air with heavenly perfume.

Complete strangers would stop to ask her, "How is it you have such a beautiful garden?"

Mrs. Mac would often invite visitors in for tea and scones and enjoyed telling them about her Willy the Worm.

"Deep deep down under my garden lives a worm I named Willy. He is the biggest and the smartest worm in the world.

He just loves taking care of the soil with the mulch I make from newspaper, cardboard and food scraps. Willy does the rest with the other smaller worms. Together they make the richest fertilizer, and that is why I have the best garden in town."

Mrs. Mac thought that, that was all there was to Willy, however there was much more to him than turning mulch into fertilizer.

Willy was indeed a big worm and he worked very hard to stay that way. Birds dreamed about having a Willy worm breakfast, but none were smart enough to catch him.

Yes Willy was smart alright, so smart that he taught all other worms his techniques of survival.

It was indeed an honor for young worms to be accepted into Willy's class. Willy was greatly respected by all creatures that lived underground; grubs, ants, spiders and many others. Every insect had its job to do in the earth.

"Dive, dive," Willy would shout, and all the young worms would burrow deep down into the earth, and watch as the beaks of the many different birds poked around trying to find a fat juicy worm for its breakfast.

Willy had safety lines marked throughout the worm tunnels all at different levels that that marked how long the birds beaks were. Magpies, Crows, Currawongs and of course the occasional Kookaburra.

Willy would tell the young worms, "Never go above these safety lines early in the morning or you will be breakfast for the birds! Wait until you feel Mrs. Mac pottering about, then you will know there are no birds in the garden."

Willy taught the young worms that newspapers, cardboard, and garden clippings were all good for worms to turn into fertilizer, and this makes the garden grow, giving the flowers and vegetables nourishment.

"Glass, tins and plastic we can do nothing with, he told the young ones. In time you will all learn this.

The humans on this Earth don't really understand how nature works or how they can work with nature. Nature will always find a way of to correct the mess humans make.
Sometimes the correction may be known as disasters. One day they may learn to live in balance with Nature. In the meantime we do our best."

"What will happen if humans don't learn Willy"? Asked a young worm.

"Then they will learn the hard way that Nature will only take so much abuse, they will learn that she will have the final word, so to speak and that will be harsh for human kind. Until then my fine young worms we have lots of mulching to do."

So off they all went singing… "A mulching we do, a mulching we will do, our mulching helps gardens to grow."

That's the reason that Mrs, Mac has the finest garden in the whole town.

Willy The Worm saves the Planet Zanaria

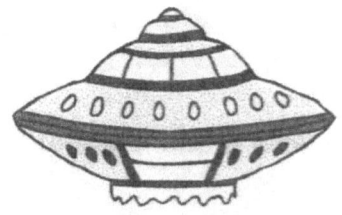

Willy The Worm saves the Planet Zanaria

Part Two

Mrs. Mac could not believe her eyes, she began to cry "where is my beautiful garden?"

People were everywhere, television cameras, reporters from newspapers and magazines.

Government officials, police and even scientists were there trying to get a look at Mrs Mac's garden, or rather the gigantic holes where the garden used to be.

"Where is your garden Mrs. Mac"? Asked the local police sergeant. "I don't know, it was there last evening." She replied.

"I have never seen anything like this in my whole life, said the sergeant scratching his head, and no one heard a sound, I find that hard to believe"

He continued to repeat himself mostly to himself, the hole in Mr. Macs garden was big enough for an Olympic size swimming pool.! It was like something had scooped her garden out very neatly and removed it without leaving any marks at all!

Even more strange her fruit trees and shrubs were also gone and it looked like there had never been any there at all! Where is my beautiful garden, how could this be done overnight without a sound?"" It was a very sad day not only for Mrs. Mac but the entire town.

Meanwhile on a tiny planet known as Zanaria there were great celebrations and excitement.

The Zanarians were expecting their spaceship to return at any moment.

Zanaria was in great trouble their planet dying, they had been inadvertently affected by the Glaxonians testing new weapons.

The Glaxonians gave no thought about how surrounding planets may be affected by their weapons.

The damage was swift, almost immediately their foliage began to die, then the soil began to dry and cracked.

Many Zanarions left to find a new planet to live on.

Those that remained began communicating with the inner world beings.

Together they devised a grand plan to save Zanaria, it had to be quick or they too would die.

They had heard from other beings of a planet called earth, how big it was, and that the humans all spoke different languages and could not communicate with inner or outer beings.

The Zanarians thought this was very strange, as only one language was spoken in their world, inner and outer. They began to gather in the centre of town and watch as their spaceship began to land.

Willy the worm stirred and thought the tremor he felt must be Mr. Jone's truck getting ready to go to the markets. He wasn't ready to get up just yet, the young worms could start without him so he curled up and went back to sleep.

"Willy, Willy wake up. Shouted the young worms. Willy there is something very wrong above. Come and see come and see."
Willy went with the young worms to see what the fuss was about.
He popped his head out of the earth and quickly slithered back down again! "Oh my oh my" said Willy rather shocked. The young worms were all huddled together shaking, knowing something was very wrong.

"Now let's not get too carried away with this. Said Willy. You young ones stay here I will sort this out" he thought to himself." I hope I can"
Willy composed himself. He went back up to the surface thinking no one would notice him and he could do some investigating.

The Zanarians were not the average type of Aliens one might expect them to be.

For as soon as Willy popped his head out a big cheer went up that shook the planet.

Willy was stunned. This was not Mrs. Macs garden! This is another world!

Coming toward him was a very official looking person, he bowed and said.

"Welcome to Zanaria we are very pleased you survived the journey"

"Why you are like our fairies, said Willy feeling much more comfortable, then in a stern voice he said. You kidnapped me AND Mrs. Macs garden!"

"I am known as Felene" he replied, and proceeded to explain why they were here.

Willy listened intently as Felene told him his story.

"That is very sad Felene, tell me how did you do it, I mean how did you get all of Mrs. Mac garden in this tiny little ship?"

Felene laughed as did everyone else, then answered."You could call it magic I suppose"

Willy liked this place, and he liked the fairy folk. He called to his young worms to join him. And said" We are here to save this planet and these people and we will all work together to do it."

"Are there any birds here Willy?" Asked a young worm. Willy in turn asked Felene.

"No replied Felene, they left long ago"

"Now that will make our work easier." Said Willy.

And so it was that Mrs. Macs garden brought new life into a tiny little planet way beyond the earth and beyond understanding.

There was no explanation about Mrs. Macs garden, no one knew where it was, no one talked about it either.

Mrs Mac started another garden, and hoped that another worm would take as good a care of it as Willy had.

As she was turning the soil of her new garden she notice a little scroll with her name on it and in one corner was a picture of a tiny planet.

Inside the scroll was a photo of her old garden along with a thank you message from the people of Zanaria and a very personal letter from Willy the Worm.

END OF STORY.

The Storyteller.

The Slumber Party.

"Mum, Could I have a slumber party this Saturday night? asked Becky Miller in her best voice. Please, please say yes" she begged as only an eight-year-old can.

Let's talk it over with your father and brother before we make plans."

Her mother replied.

"A slumber party!...Yuk!" Young Mike Miller was not impressed with the idea of a bunch of eight year old girls invading the house.

"Now come on Mike, said his father. I think it's a good idea, after all we are new to this neighbourhood, and it's a good way for your sister to make new friends."

"Well I don't want to be here when they come!" said Mike.

"Why don't we go fishing then, we could camp out overnight and the girls could have the house to themselves." said his father.

"Sam Miller, you big chicken!" said his wife. Wondering how she was going to handle the girls on her own.

"Don't worry mum, said Mike enthusiastically, you can do anything. We'll bring home lots of fish for you to cook!"

Everyone got busy in the Miller household, Mike and his Dad were gathering up all that they would need for their fishing trip, while Becky and her Mum cleared the lounge room for the sleeping bags.

"How many girls are coming Becky?" asked her Mum.

"Oh, maybe five or six." Becky replied.

Saturday came very quickly; Mike and his Dad had left very early in the morning long before Becky and her Mum were out of bed.

By four o'clock everything was ready for the Slumber Party.

There were more than five or six girls though. Becky had invited her whole class! She didn't think they would all turn up!

Mrs. Miller stayed in the background while keeping a discreet eye on them and letting the girls do their own thing.

Mrs. Miller had a way with children, they were instantly relaxed around her.

Everyone helped with getting dinner ready and clearing up too.

The girls gathered in the lounge room and Mrs. Miller served them all hot chocolate and marshmallows. They sang songs and talked about what they wanted to do when they grew up.

"Mum, what did you do when you were a little girl, without Television or Mobile phones?"

The girls repeated Becky's sentence followed with a "Really"!

Mrs. Miller smiled and replied. "We used to listen to our nana tell stories, she was a good storyteller"

"Did you have a favourite one Mrs. Miller?" asked Sally Williams.

"Yes I did, my very favourite one was about a wood chopper."

"Oooh, would you tell us that one please Mrs. Miller." Asked a bright-eyed Bethany Cox.

"I'd love to Bethany. Becky dim the lights please."

They all gathered around in excited expectation.

"Has anyone heard of Sherwood Forest?" asked Mrs. Miller.

Yes, came the reply.

"That's where Robin Hood lived," said sally.

"That's right, said Mrs. Miller, Robin Hood was not the only person living in those woods. Many people lived there.

The least talked about one was a woodchopper and his family. He would cut the trees and prepare the wood for sale to the town folk. They in turn would make tables, chairs and build cabins and logs for cooking.

The people of that time relied on the forest to supply all their needs. Not only wood but also deer rabbits and fruit.

The woodchopper's name was Joe. He could not read or write, he was a very hard man

He made his wife and children work hard too.

The children never had time to play games or have fun. Joe was always angry and he drank too much wine.

One day Joe came home very angry and very drunk, more than usual.

He had not made as much money as he thought he would.

When his family heard him cursing, they ran off into the woods, knowing if they stayed, they would feel his belt across their backs!

Joe kicked in the front door and yelled "Where's my dinner, where's my damn dinner you useless woman!"

He was met with a silence that made him angrier." What a miserable excuse I have for a family! He yelled at the top of his voice."

He became so enraged that he grabbed his axe and started to chop up his own house.

Then he went into the forest cursing, axe in one hand and bottle of wine in the other chopping down everything that was in his way old trees, young trees, not caring for the damage he was causing. He was like a mad man, becoming so exhausted and falling into a drunken sleep.

Darkness crept over the forest, a strange darkness, so still and quiet, like the stillness in a graveyard. There was no movement, not a whisper. The sound of a drunken woodchopper moaning and groaning sent an earie vibration through the forest.

Joe stirred and tried to stand up only to fall down again, he could do nothing but lay in the darkness, a darkness he had never seen before. He drank some more wine and cursed some more.

Suddenly piercing through the forest was a bright light, so bright that it hurt Joes eyes.

He tried to focus on the light and just managed to get up on his feet although very unsteady, he began muttering to himself. Then in the light he saw a giant figure coming towards him.

He rubbed his eyes and yelled, "Who are you, what are you?" without waiting for an answer he yelled. "WHATEVER YOU ARE GET OUT OF MY FOREST……. now!"

"Your Forest!" came the booming reply. "This Forest does not belong to you"

Joe swung his axe at the figure but it went straight through it.

"Show yourself you mangey coward so I can chop you into pieces!"

"Any one want some hot chocolate" asked Mrs. Miller.

A chorus of NO rang out," keep going please, what happened next?"

Laughter rang through the forest; the wind began to howl moving with it's might the surrounding trees. The leaves began to laugh as the wind played its game with them.

Around and around went the wind picking up all the leaves on the forest floor and throwing them up in the air like the clowns at the circus with their coloured balls.

Joe swung at the figure again and again, each time the axe went straight through, he swung again so hard that he fell over, cursing he yelled "What manner of man are you that I cannot kill!"

The answer boomed through the forest...."I am no manner of man, I am the guardian of this forest and you woodchopper are no longer welcome here. You have destroyed trees unnecessarily; they have provided you with so much and this is how you thank them!"

"I don't know what you are talking about, they are just dumb trees, I don't have to thank them, anyone would think they have feelings!' with that Joe swung his axe and cut off a branch of a nearby tree, it lifted high into the air like an arrow and came back down into Joe's arm cutting him deeply. Joe screamed in pain.

"That's how a tree feels when you chop it down in anger" said the guardian of the forest.

Joe went crazy, swinging his axe blindly each time Joe cut into a tree a part of the tree would embed itself in Joes body. The wind picked up a branch and threw it at Joe pinning him to the ground, then the wind gathered up all the leaves and completely covered Joes body until it could not be seen.

The night began to fade and the sun crept over the forest touching the trees with gentleness bringing warmth and new life into the forest.

Birds sang their greetings to the new day as the animals began to wake up and the flowers began to open, bringing their fragrances and colour into the forest. A rainbow appeared briefly through the morning mist and Sherwood Forest was peaceful once more.

The woodchopper's family stood quietly looking at what was left of their house, they looked at each other and then looked at the forest.

"I don't think your father is coming home anymore" said Joes wife.

"The forest looks different today doesn't it Ma." said the children.

"That it does, that it does."

The village folk spent a good week looking for Joe, there was no trace of him anywhere, it was if the forest had swallowed him. Joe was never seen again.

The woodchopper's family moved away from Sherwood Forest, for at night the ghostly sounds of cursing and of laughter frightened them and the voices they heard in the wind and the bright light that could not be explained was just too much for them.

They moved to another village where the children could play and be happy.

"How was your slumber party Becky?" asked her father

"It was the best Dad; did you catch any fish?"

"We sure did, replied her brother. We went night fishing; boy was that scary."

"I bet it's not as scary as Sherwood Forest is at night" said Becky making ghostly sounds.

"What's Sherwood Forest got to do with fishing." asked her father.

"Nothing at all," said Mrs. Miller. Making ghostly sounds with Becky.

Monday afternoon Becky came home from school very excited." Mum, guess what?

She was so excited she could not stand still. Before her mother could say anything, Becky continued.

We started a special group at school today and my class is in charge, our group is called the Tree Keepers' and it is our responsibility to make sure the trees in the school grounds are looked after, I mean REALLY looked after because trees are really important, it's all because of the story you told of the woodchopper.

Bethany Cox told Miss Courtney all about it and Miss Courtney was very impressed and she said you should write a book about it, then every one would know about how important trees are."

"Maybe one day I just might." Said Mrs. Miller.

"I am so happy Mum everyone wants to be my friend now. When can I have another slumber party?"

End.

The Bracelet

"If any part of this story relates to any living or
deceased person, it is purely coincidental."

This is a story about friendship love and the unexplainable.

Casey and Timiki are best friends. They first met in 5th Grade.

Holidaying in Japan they experience magic and for a short time

A dream becomes a reality.

The Dream.

Casey sat in the waiting room of Naomi Henderson Dream psychologist. Then she changed her mind and was about to leave when the door opened. There stood a very tall, elegant woman with long auburn hair that fell perfectly around her shoulders like a cape. She smiled at Casey as if she knew she was about to leave.

"Come in Casey, and make yourself comfortable. How can I help you?"

"I have been having a re-occurring dream and I wondered if you could tell me what it means. I don't usually remember dreams, but this one upsets me."

"Tell me about it Casey, relax and take your time."

'Well, in the dream I am a Japanese girl. I am standing in a glasshouse taking care of the Bonsai plants, there are many to take care of, maybe forty or more. I am singing and appear to be very happy. It is like watching a movie.

Casey went into great detail of what she was wearing, the scenery outside, and how small her feet were.

Then a man comes in and tells me he has a gift for me. He is so good-looking and is dressed up like a Samurai. Then I wake up feeling very sad."

"Why do you think you feel sad Casey?" asked Naomi.

"Because I didn't get to see the gift!"

Casey had tears in her eyes she knew it was more than the gift that made her sad, what else was there to know.

"The mind can be very intense at times Casey. There is so much to learn about its secrets. Have you ever thought about having a past life regression?"

"NO. I came here for a dream interpretation, isn't that what you do. I am not into regression and I don't believe in past life anything!"

"It was only a suggestion Casey. The dream could be a romantic yearning, triggered off by a Movie you have seen."

Casey did not hear anything else, her mind took her back to the glass house.

"Casey, you are not listening to me!" Naomi's voice was sharp, Casey blinked a little startled. Being here is a mistake she thought.

"Yes, you are probably right. It could be just a yearning, you never know, there may be a second part to the dream where I get the gift."

"If you do have a dream where you get the gift I would be interested in knowing about it."

"Sure." said Casey paying at the reception and left.

Friendship.

Casey walked to Circular Quay, her favourite place in Sydney, and just walked around looking at the water and watching the Ferries go by.

Many people from all over the world came to the 'Quay (as it was known and pronounced as Key). Although it was a very busy place Casey found peace being there.

Casey loved living in Sydney, to her it was alive and vibrant. Everything she wanted was right here.

Hearing her name called, Casey turned around to see the smiling face of her best friend Timiki.

Friday nights Timiki and Casey would eat out and go to the movies or go to Caseys Apartment and just talk.

Casey and Timiki had been friends since fifth grade Primary school. Casey had befriended Timiki from being picked on because she was different.

"I am an Australian," Timiki cried, "I was born here!" trying to make herself heard over the chorus of "Jap, Jap, shut your trap."

Casey stood in front of the Headmistress Mrs. Walker.

"Girls do not fight in this school, Cassandra Mathews. You are on detention for the next week, and you can write 50 times out every day Girls do not fight!"

Casey had told her why she was fighting. However rules were rules that must be followed. There was no excuse for such behavior.

From then on Casey and Timiki were inseparable.

"Kon nichiwa Ogenki Des Ka Onisan." Casey greeted Timikis parents, then quickly apologising for her not very good Japanese.

Mr. Utako replied, G'day Casey, and they all laughed.

"It is only important that one tries Casey."

Mr. Utako was such a gentle man. He always spoke softly. He was a caring man, who loved his family, that is what Casey saw, a loving family.

"You are in much trouble at school Casey."

It's alright, Mrs. Utako, the week will go quickly, and besides it was worth it."

"People all over the world sometimes behave badly towards other people that are different to them, I doubt that this will change any time soon. Fighting will not change it either. We are grateful that you came to our daughters assistance, but please do not fight again."

"Oh I don't have to Mrs. Utako, nobody picks on Timiki anymore. My mum says some people are just plain rude, my Dad put in an official complaint as well, he said the other girls should have been disciplined for their bad behavior."

It didn't take the school long to respond, Mr. and Mrs. Utako received an official letter apologising for the distress the incident may have caused their daughter assuring them it would never happen again.

Both families became good friends, exchanging stories from Japan and Bush Tales from Australia, and of course food.

The years went by quickly. Now both girls were 24 years old and still good friends. "Timiki, have you ever thought how ironic it is that we have so much in common? Like we share the same birthday, we like the same colours, food, so much about us is the same."

"Well, that makes us unique doesn't it. What did the psychologist say about your dream?"

"She said that the mind is very intense! And I could be just yearning for love! I paid good money for that information, it was a mistake going there, and she yelled at me too!"

Mum said the same thing, and she didn't yell at me.

My mum says if you have the same dream more than once, then there is something you have to do, and you will keep having the dream until you do it.

Maybe your mum and mine should be Psychologist. They make more sense and they could become rich as well!

Something will happen and you will know what you have to do.

Well I can tell you that it won't be a past life regression!

The Journey.

"Casey, let's go to Japan. We could stay with my fathers parents, and you never know what may happen." Timiki said with a grin.

"What will your parents think of you taking off on such an adventure with a wild girl like me.

My parents love you Casey, You are their number two daughter. They know we will look after each other. Besides I have already talked to them about going, and they are happy that I want to go, my Grandparents will be happy too.

"Let's do it." Casey was excited at the prospect of visiting Japan, it had to be a good place, Timiki said it was and that was good enough for her.

That afternoon and evening Timiki and Casey began making travel plans, when was the best time to go, how long they would stay. They wrote a list out just to make sure they wouldn't forget anything.

"Where do your grandparents live?"

"Okinawa. It is said that Okinawa is a very mystical place, it is beautiful all year round. I have only been there once, when I was 3 years old so I don't remember much about it."

"Hmmmm, mystical you say."

Hmmmm, mystical they said together and laughed.

"Remember the barbeque on Sunday, your parents are still coming aren't they?"

"Would not miss it for the world. My mum loves being spoilt by your mum."

Barbeques at the Utako's was always a wonderful experience. One never knew what to expect.

Life had been good for Yashiro and Tatomi, here in their Woolwich home. They had both worked hard to fit in and be accepted, and they were. Success had not changed these people. They were gentle and fun-loving, they had a great sense of humor.

Casey arrived early on Sunday afternoon to help prepare to help setting up chairs. Mostly sampling the food and asking questions about how was this or that was made.

The doorbell rang, Ron and June Mathews had arrived, they were greeted with sheer delight, and treated like long lost friends each time they visited.

"So, Yashiro, our girls are going to Japan, How do you feel about it," asked Ron.

"Well, Ron, at first I was concerned. I feel the same as you, no matter how old my daughter is, I still think of her as my little girl.

My wife (being very wise) pointed out to me that we have taught our daughter right from wrong. We have taught her well. She is sensible and intelligent, as is your daughter, they will be alright.

However we as parents will do as all parents do when their children are travelling overseas and that my friend is to worry!"

Ron smiled, "We can worry together my friend."

"You would have to work hard at worrying here, with this beautiful view." said June as she helped Tatomi with pre-dinner snacks.

Casey and Timiki spent the next week getting organised.

"You won't need all those clothes Casey. I am sure you will be able to buy some really trendy clothes in Japan."

"I don't want to be short of anything mum."

Casey's mum didn't push her she knew her daughter was feeling nervous and excited.

"Just remember you will have to pay for excess luggage."

Casey re-packed her bags.

The day of departure came quickly, Casey and Timiki arrived at the International Airport in Sydney three hours before their flight, just in case the plane left early.

Then it was time to board.

Last minute apprehension was experienced by both the girls and their parents.

"Just one more hug," said Casey with tears in her eyes and butterflies in her stomach.

Casey performed a final farewell. Waving her arms and attracting the attention of fellow traveler's. Bowing she said quiet loudly." Farewell my Mother and Father, keep safe until my return!"

That's my girl, said her father.

Mine too! Said Timiki's father.

Okinawa.

In just over twelve hours Casey and Timiki arrived in Okinawa.

A strange feeling went through Casey as she looked around this subtropical place.

Timiki's Grandparents were very excited at having their granddaughter visit them and honored that she brought a friend with her.

Hajime Mashite (how do you do.) Doozo Yoroshiku (nice to meet you) Casey greeted. Yashiro and Mayumi Utako.

"Well done Casey!" said Timiki upon introducing Casey to her Grandparents.

"You may call me Grandmother Mayumi, Casey."

"You can also call me Grandfather Yashiro."

"That's quiet an honor Casey, it means you are welcomed into the family."

"Okinawa is a popular destination, Casey. Most everyone can speak and understand English." said Yasiro.

"What a relief," said Casey, "my Japanese is not real good."

"My son has told me much about you Casey, I hope you will take home some happy memories from your visit with us."

The following week was spent looking around, Yashiro and Mayumi were delighted in showing off their Granddaughter as all good Grandparents do.

The Glass House.

Casey sat on the verandah looking out over the emerald sea surrounding this magical place, then yelled out to Timiki that she was going for a walk by herself.

As she strolled down towards the beach she noticed a glass house. She didn't know that Timiki's Grandfather had one.

Opening the door she stepped in and noticed there were at least fifty Bonsai plants! There were so many different shapes and sizes, this is amazing she thought.

Then she started singing softly. At that moment she became aware she was wearing a Kimino and her feet were very small. She was no longer Casey nor was she in the twentieth century!

"Tomasita, at last I have found you!"

Such joy filled her heart as she embraced her husband. Tomashun. So many months he had been away.

From his pocket he pulled out a glass box. Inside was the most beautiful delicate gold chain bracelet Tomasita had ever seen.

"This my love was made especially for you from the finest craftsman in all of Japan, there is no other like it. This is the only one, I was going to give it to you in your twenty fourth birthday, but I was too late. This bracelet is unique for when it goes on, the clip disappears, so it looks like one piece. People will wonder how you got it on. Like my love for you it can never be removed.

As Tomashun was putting the bracelet on her tiny wrist, she told him of the loss of their son at birth, of how she had called his name over and over again to give her strength. Of how she became lost in the darkness of sadness for a very long time. They both cried together. He cradled her in his arms, vowing his love for her and declaring that he would never leave her alone again.

With this bracelet I will always be with you, neither time nor space will separate us.

"Casey, Casey where are you?"

"I am here Timiki," a dazed Casey answered not sure what had just happened.

"I have been looking for you for two hours! I was so worried."

"I didn't know your grandfather had a glass house." Casey told Timiki what had just happened and showed her the bracelet.

"Oh Casey it is so beautiful and unusual, there is no clip, and the links are so small. It looks like one piece of gold."

"Grandfather Yashiro, Your glass house is beautiful, the Bonsai are so perfect."

Yashiro looked shocked. "I have no glass house Casey, the only Bonsai I have is in the dining room."

Mayumi put her arms around Casey. "This is a magical place Casey, sometimes the unexplainable happens."

Mayumi didn't seem at all surprised at what had just happened.

Before leaving Okinawa Casey and Timiki visited the Shurijo Castle in Naha city. The castle was the residence of the Ryuku royal family for about 450 years from the 15th century. It was stunning and they spent most of the day there. From here they had a panoramic view of Naha city and the East China Sea.

"The atmosphere here is very strong Timiki. It's like stepping back in time."

"Yes I feel it too. Speaking of time, we have to go Casey."

Sayonara Grandfather Yashiro. Sayonara Grandmother Mayumi. Thank you both for having me. I take home many happy memories.

Casey gave them a photo of her and Timiki at the entrance of Shurijo Castle with Casey dressed in a Kimino and Timiki dressed in jeans and a T-shirt with I am an Aussie girl on the front.

"I think we will need another case just for the photo's." Timiki said. There was a sadness about leaving Okinawa for both Casey and Timiki.

Before heading home to Australia they spent three wonderful days and two nights in Tokyo.

"We need at least six months here," said Casey. "There is so much to see and do."

The Power of Love.

"It feels good to be going home, I will never forget Okinawa or what happened to me there." said Casey.

"Are you going to tell your parents about it Casey?"

"No."

"Back to work on Monday, I wonder if anything has changed."

"Maybe I'll have a coffee machine in my office". said Casey.

You wish!

On the tenth floor was Martin Conrad's Law Firm. Casey's office looked out over Sydney Harbour.

Coffee in hand she sat down at her desk, with a sigh and looked out her window, wondering what else life was going to present her with, it would have to be pretty spectacular to be better than what she had experienced in The Glass House!

"Welcome back Casey. We all missed you. How was your holiday," asked Martin Conrad as he gave her a bunch of Daffodils.

"Oh, thank you Marty, they are beautiful. I had a wonderful holiday. Anything change while I was away?"

"Yes, I'd like you to meet someone, I've taken on a partner. This is something I've been thinking about for some time. Martin Conrad's Law Firm is now Conrad and Shanshi International Law Firm. I believe it is a first of its kind."

"Wow, you have been busy."

"Sam, I'd like to introduce you to our number one secretary, Cassandra Mathews, she knows all there is about the running of this firm."

"Pleased to meet you Cassandra."

"Everyone calls me Casey, Pleased to meet you too." Casey looked at the tall good looking man in front of her and felt weak in her knees.

"Where abouts in Japan do you come from Mr. Sanshi?"

"Please call me Sam, I was born in Nagasaki, I was eight when my family came to live in Australia. He smiled, then added, my father named me Sam after our ancestor who was a great Samuri."

"Casey I have to go out, will you show Sam around so he can familiarise himself as to where everything is. I'll be back in a couple of hours."

"OK."

"That's an unusual braceret you have, do you mind my asking you where you got it from?"

"It was a gift."

"Lets go and have something to eat, suggested Sam. After all it's your first day back at work and mine too so we will take it easy."

"Sounds good to me." I like this man, casey thought to herself.

Sam again commented on the bracelet." It is very strange, one exactly like that has been handed down through my family since the 15ᵗʰ century, I believed it was the only one like it in the world.

"Really," said Casey starting to feel weak in her knees again. She cleared her throat. "Sounds fascinating, tell me more."

"It was in a glass box locked in a vault, it lay on a golden silk pillow. There is a scroll with it written by my ancestor a Samuri known as Tomashun, it tells of a lost love, his wife who died during childbirth while he was away. He vowed he would find her. He alone had the key to open the box. When he would find her he would put the bracelet on her and it would become one piece, no clip. What is even stranger is two weeks ago my father dreamed the box had been opened and the bracelet was removed. He went straight to the vault and found it still locked, but no bracelet, it had vanished."

"Sometimes," said Casey, "the unexplainable happens and there is nothing one can do about it."

"Maybe," said Sam, "I believe that when the time is right the truth presents itself."

The day went slowly and finally it was time to go home. She felt very tired as she lay on her bed thinking of what Sam had told her.

Falling into a deep sleep, she dreams she was back in the glass house, not in Okinawa though. It was in the foyer of Conrad and Sanshi International Law Firm! Turning around she sees Sam walking towards her.

Then she wakes up.

www.ingramcontent.com/pod-product-compliance
Lightning Source LLC
Chambersburg PA
CBHW031217120626
46545CB00003B/887